This and That

K.T. STEVENS

PublishAmerica
Baltimore

© 2012 by K.T. Stevens.
All rights reserved. No part of this book may be reproduced, stored in a retrieval system or transmitted in any form or by any means without the prior written permission of the publishers, except by a reviewer who may quote brief passages in a review to be printed in a newspaper, magazine or journal.

First printing

PublishAmerica has allowed this work to remain exactly as the author intended, verbatim, without editorial input.

Softcover 9781462654352
PUBLISHED BY PUBLISHAMERICA, LLLP
www.publishamerica.com
Baltimore

Printed in the United States of America

Recognition to:

My husband, for his patience and assistance in bringing my rhymes to completion.

To God for His Inspiration.

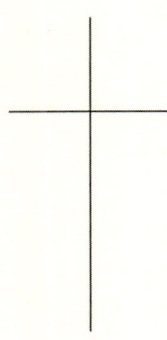

...

You will notice that throughout this book you will find

rhymes taken from my other books and

inserted into the contents.

This was done to give you a glimpse into the contents of my other books,

and hopefully make you want to read them as well.

I hope you enjoy reading what is between the covers of this book.

...

To My Readers

My books are unique in that they are not your typical book of rhymes

I write short stories (2-3 pages) and one page opinions, thoughts as well as one page stories…all in rhyme.

Some are based on my own personal experiences in life and others are things I have observed, and others are simply made up.

I have tired not to offend anyone with my opinions, but I do remind my readers that they are simply that—my opinions.

I would like to think that my readers will see their own opinions in mine, and say, "Well I am glad I am not the only one who thinks that way!"

It is like having a conversation over coffee with all my readers and we are discussing different topics.

K.T. Stevens

…

K.T. Stevens

Our Four Legged Friends

She didn't really mind being in her kennel.
In fact she often went in there on her own and took naps.
But because she was so obliging,
When it was necessary for her to be in her kennel
And have the door closed…
She sometimes would growl in protest!

I personally believe she was just expressing
Her thoughts on the subject and wanted the door left open.
So her human parents tried that and she was very good.
When they returned home, they found her where they had left her…
In the kennel asleep.

Some people don't appreciate how smart their pets are.
I know that we, and several other people,
Have to spell certain things because our dogs
Understand so much of what we say and do.

They are the best friend a person can have.
They try to please us.
They DO talk back;
But we can handle that.

They know when we are feeling down.
They go through grieving just like we do.
And best of all…They don't judge us.
They love us for who we are.

So if you are a Good Pet Parent…
GOOD FOR YOU!!!

Keep it up.
God put our four legged friends on this earth for us.
Treat them well…
Or St. Frances may see to it that in the after life
You don't fair so well!!!

…

Now and Then

Her philosophy was that she
Had been around long enough
And seen everything there was to see.
She said there was very little that could surprise her
At this stage in her life!

On the other hand…
She would often say, "Now I have seen everything!"

The world changes constantly.
It always has and always will.
That is something to bet on—as a done deal!

People aren't so different now—than they were way back when.
It is just that there are more of us now.
Things we really didn't think about before are now thrown in our face!

We now have more access to the electronic world.
Nothing goes on without everyone hearing about it.
And I do mean nothing!

What we need to do is to concentrate
On the senior citizens of our time.
Ask them questions;
Let them tell us about what it was like when they were growing up.

We can't appreciate going forward,
Unless we know where we have been!!

…

I am the same as you!

I am a little girl,
I am fun, smart, and **witty**.
But when other children look at me,
They shutter and say **icky!**

One minute I was having fun running and jumping…
The next thing I remember is falling into the bon-fire.
I now bear those scars and will for the rest of my **life**.
But I am not going to give up without a **fight!**

I look sort of funny, and I have no **hair**.
My face is scared, which causes some to **stare!**

We are all different in our own **way**.
That is what makes us unique;
It's not a reason to stay **away**.
Please won't you come over and **play?**

Inside I am the same as **you**…
And I would love it if you could see that **too!**

…

(*From "Rhymes for Our Serious Side"*)

The Grumpy Old Man

I once knew a man who was jolly and **pleasant**.
As time went on his personality was on a rapid **decent!**

He wasn't really that 'old' in years;
He just acted like **it.**
I could no longer handle it…not for another **minute!**

I stayed my distance,
And I really didn't miss the new him much.
I liked him better when he was jolly and **pleasant.**
This change in our relationship was not worth the **investment!**

I still see him from time to time while he is on his morning walk.
I wave as I pass him by.
He looks up and gives me a go away or never mind type wave **back.**
Like I said, on friendliness—his personality does **lack!**

Of his personality I don't really mean to **attack.**
I will cut him some **slack.**
But I just wish his old personality would come **back!!**

…

She Is Who She Is

I once knew a lady who was a hard worker.
The problem was that she didn't know when it was time to **stop**.
She would go and go until whatever it was she was doing was done.
She worked until she was about to **drop**.
She couldn't help it though.
Then in a couple days, one or **two**—
She was done in for.
Sometimes she couldn't even **move!**

It was all part of this thing they call O.C.D.
Obsessive Compulsive Disorder!

She wasn't as bad as some who also have this **condition;**
But she had a problem…by her own **admission!**

This 'condition' as it is called, had its plusses **too.**
She could out work me and you!

…

Homosexuality

This is not a rhyme per-say;
But rather a definition of the word **'Gay'**.

It has been defined by many…
And is usually just 'what they personally have to say.
Let's look at it from a medical view point.

And now, please hear what I personally have to say!!

Why is that babies are born with many abnormalities and they are just accepted with those…abnormalities?

I am not saying that homosexuality is an abnormality…
or maybe I am!

We all know that the human body is made up of many genes, cells and hormones.

Sometimes these get mixed up when developing into the human person.

A person can be born without a hand or an arm.

A person can be born blind.

A person can even be born with a hole in their heart.

People are born with birthmarks, hair lips, and facial deformities.

Conjoined twins…even a single body with two heads!!

So tell me why then is it that people think that a homosexual **"picks"** or **"chooses"** their way of life?

Did the people listed above choose to have their unusual characteristics?

I know that we are to believe that God thinks of this life style as a sin.

I don't believe that to be true.

God is good and God is kind.

God made you and me **and 'them'!**

Each birth is a miracle…Not an accident.

How you are born and what you are
Is determined in the womb…
Not after you start or live your life!!

You are who and what you are.

…

(From "Rhymes for Our Serious Side")

Interpretation
(While we are on the subject…)

The bible is unique in that each person can interpret the words to meet their own needs.

The bible was written 'after the fact', and written in that person's own words or interpretation.

Therefore, the gospels have to be taken "with a grain of salt", as the saying goes.

They were written in a manner so that the people of that time could understand them.

They made up stories to interpret a meaning they wanted to get across.

For example, "I personally" don't believe that there was ever Adam and Eve and a Garden of Eden.

It just doesn't make sense!

My point is that God was wise enough to give us a brain and 'free will'.

We must use both of these when interpreting what we are taught and what we are taught to believe.

A person who loves another of the same sex is not 'sick, sinful, or disturbed'!

It may not seem natural to you…
But then are the abnormalities listed earlier natural?

We live with what God gave us!

Disabilities, Brains, Beauty, etc.

God apparently wanted us to live the way he made us,
Or he wouldn't have made us that way.

You don't choose to be attracted to the same sex.

But it sure beats being drawn to the opposite sex
just for society's sake and being unhappy.

Many young people who feel this way are afraid to show it.
They end up using drugs or alcohol to get by.

When you see on the news that the homosexual society wants
the right
to be 'married'…
Don't get yourself all upset!

"I personally" don't believe they should be united in a
"marriage" either…
However what I do believe (and you should too), is that they
have a right to a
Commitment Ceremony!!

What this would give them is the right to see their partner in situations that a married couple would.

Examples would be to be able to be at the bedside of their dying partner.
The privileges of a family member.
Joint insurance coverage, etc.

I believe this is all they are really fighting for.

So the next time you feel like raising your eye brows,
Or making a snide remark…
Don't!!

They are just like you and me, only with different preferences!

God created each and every one of us…
Let's make him proud!!!

…

(From "Rhymes for Our Serious Side)

The Dog that Growled

My friend had a dog…
This dog was very **small**
And as for people—he growled at them **all!**

But when left with its owners this little dog was an angel.
Some might say an angel with **horns!**
But one thing was for sure…
This little dog—they did so **adore!**

It was just the dog's nature.
It didn't see many people
And when it was out and about,
It was contained in a carrier…never **interacting.**
Her personality…will be **everlasting!!**

…

"Not Other Things!"

We recently went on vacation to **see**
Tennessee!

We accepted an **offer,**
And stayed with our **daughter!**

She and her partner have several house **cats**
who after investigating and hiding, finally sat on our **laps!**

One in particular enjoyed sleeping at the top of my **head,**
Into which her paws she did **spread!**

My hair is short, but that was no **matter,**
For she managed to nest right down and get it all **matted!**

When I got up in the mornings,
I had to explain…
"It was the cat! Not other things!!"

…

(From "A Smile in Rhyme)

While He Was Away…

She sent him off on his trip
Knowing full well that he would be missed.

He was gone for over two **weeks**.
It was a surprise to her that staying alone
did not give her the **creeps!**

She kept herself very busy in his absence.
She had some chores that she had put on **hold**
for just such a time when she would be **alone**.

She painted, she scrubbed, and she took on every project
there could **be**.
One was way beyond her area of **expertise**.

She (with help) cleared out their bedroom,
Pulled up the carpet and padding and
A N D
Wait for It!…
And then she laid down tile…all by **herself!**
She was so proud she shouted…
I did it all by **myself!**

This was all unbeknown to her traveling husband.
Upon his return he was surprised…
Surprised at the changes, but also at the pile of
Receipts she left for him on his **desk**.
She had them all in a neat pile…
She didn't like a **mess**.
His comment on all her changes
Was simply that taking his trip…was something he did not **regret!**

He knew she possessed skills beyond what she was **aware.**
And next time he travels, he will be curious what other changes
She could possibly make to their house
While he is totally **unaware!!**

...

Aging

Once you were strong and **healthy**.
Now you tend to swear at the **Almighty**!

For what you were capable of doing at **26**,
you now find a chore to accomplish
anything below the **neck**!

What you once did without even thinking,
You can only do now after much "rethinking"!

When you were young you could put your foot into the
Bathroom sink.

Now you have to strain and **tug**
Just to get it into the bathroom **tub**!

Age has its advantages **too**.
Now you can forget something
And nobody blames **you**.
People don't expect as much from **you**;
And they are impressed by whatever you **do**!

When you are young, you are expected to be thin and **fit**.
But as you age, if you are **thin**…
They are worried you will fall and break a **hip**!

You get to do your exercises in a swimming pool,
Or even better; sitting **down**.
It is grand that this is **allowed**!

You can pass **gas,**
And those around quietly **laugh!**

The funny thing about aging is that although
Your body is old on the outside,
Your mind (or what you have left of it),
Stays young on the inside!

You want to do the things you did when you were young,
The problem is that your body and your mind
are not always on the same **page.**
That is my description of old age!!

...

(From "Rhymes for Our Serious Side")

The Beautiful Garden

Once upon a time there was an elderly lady who lived alone.
She was the best gardener in the **land**.
Some said that instead of a green thumb…
She had a green **hand!**

There was also an elderly man who walked his dog
Every morning and **night**.
He would walk right past the lady's house and admired her flowers.
In the morning he would see her pruning and weeding.
At night he would watch as she watered her garden.
In conversation he did try to engage her with all his **might!**

He discovered she was just hard of hearing.
And once that was established;
He started visiting with her as he passed **by.**
He would have liked a more personal friendship;
On that he would not **lie**.
He settled for her friendship and admired her garden.
For her garden was beautiful and caught everyone's **eye.**
As time went on he saw less and less of this lady…
This lady who he so enjoyed visiting in her garden as he passed **by!**

He made inquiries and was told that she was ill
And no longer was able to care for her beloved flowers.
He did what he knew he had to do…
Every morning he visited her garden and pulled weeds,
And pruned and watered.

She would watch him from her window, wave and **smile.**
He was doing something he knew pleased her…
And he smiled all the **while!**

Then one day she was gone…from the house and this world.
She was in heaven enjoying the most beautiful garden there ever was.
Soon there was a for sale sign in the yard.
He continued to care for his friend's garden until the house **sold**.
He thought of it as his garden now…if truth be **told**!

When the new tenants moved in, they neglected this beautiful garden.
Weeds were growing up everywhere and things were getting out of control!

He approached the new neighbors and told them the story of the garden.
He said he knew he was getting **old**,
But he said if he could be so **bold**…
He would like to continue taking care of the **garden**
For his friend would be watching from **heaven**
And to have it go amuck would give her such distress!

Well the lady of the house wasn't sure she wanted a stranger
Working in her yard and she told him **so**.
And she told him she didn't have much **dough**!

He said he didn't want **money**…
He wanted to do it for his dear friend's **memory**!

She agreed on one condition—That he would teach her how to maintain this lovely garden.
They could work on it together!

So along with the lady,
The elderly man cleaned up the garden.
They continued to work on it together until he was no longer able.
When he left, he knew he was leaving it in good hands!

After that, he and his friend tended to God's Garden…
The greenest best garden of all.
And they spent the rest of eternity TOGETH**ER**
Which is what he wanted…just to be with **her!!**

…

The Mess on His Desk

He kept a calendar on his **desk**…
The desk which is ALWAYS a **mess**.
Of him, I expected no **less!**

I don't know why he kept a calendar on his **desk**…
He could never find it…in all that **mess**.
The desk which is ALWAYS a **mess**.

I talked to him about his **mess**…
The mess which is on his **desk!**

He just simply said, "Give it a **rest!**"
"I don't want to discuss this mess on my **desk!**"
The desk which is ALWAYS a **mess!**

He said he was as productive as all the **rest,**
And he knew where everything was
On the desk which is ALWAYS a **mess!**

So I now watch from a distance and keep an eye on his **desk**…
The desk which is ALWAYS a **mess**.
Of him, I expected no **less!!**

…

Snore? Who Me!

As I lay here and listen to your **snore,**
It is loud enough to knock the hinges off the bedroom **door!**

I would get up,
but my movement would make the bed **shake...**
Causing you to **awake!**

Instead I will lie by your **side**
Until morning **arrives!**

Then tomorrow night, we can **begin**
all over **again!!**

...

Indecision

She wanted to go places and do **things**.
She also wanted to stay home and enjoy her own **things**.
She had a dilemma when it came to these types of **things**!

She enjoyed **entertaining**.
And she enjoyed **attending**.
She had a hard decision in **deciding**!

She was more of a **watcher**—
than a **marcher**.

She was ok with being **alone**.
To large groups she was not **prone**.
She just liked staying at **home**.

At home she wanted to go on vacation.
On vacation, she wanted to be **home**.
For at **home**
She was **prone**
To stay there all **alone**!

She had a dilemma when it came to these types of things!!

...

True Love

Once upon a time there was a very beautiful young **girl**.
She was promised to a rich merchant and was to become his wife.
Of this, she was upset and just wanted to **hurl!**

The merchant was nice, but also was many years older than **her**.
Even his money and status were not enough.
She was in love with a candle stick **maker!**

Well she had no way **out**.
It did not matter how much she did **shout!**

She had to go through with **it**.
Her parents told her love would come and until then
She would just have to make the best of **it**
and stop throwing these **fits!**

She did not know what to **do**.
When her wedding day came,
She pretended to have the **flu**.
But better then this, they all **knew!**

What to do?
What to do?

So before the ceremony she sent a **note**
(via her maid) to her love, the candle stick maker.
She told him to join her at the dock by his **boat!**

She knew that by running **away**
She could keep these wedding plans at **bay**.
She had no intentions of that day being her wedding **day!**

When she saw him, she ran into his open **arms**.
Of course there was cause for **alarm**.

They had to make sail **immediately**.
They did so not knowing their **destiny!**

Well her parents were filled with shame.
Their family name had been disgraced.
Her to-be groom's ego was **deflated**.
But with the result, the young girl was **elated!**

She was sad that she could never again return to her **home**.
At times she felt all **alone!**

But she had married her true **love**.
They made their home across the ocean.
She sent messages to her parents by
Pigeon and **Dove**.
They lived happily ever after…
With their undying **love!!**

Her love, the candle stick maker!!

…

Crazy Sadie

There once was a **lady**.
Her name was **Sadie!**

The problem was that **Sadie**
was just plain **Crazy!**

She was the talk of the **town**.
The kids would torment her when she went into **town**.
They called her *Crazy Sadie* as they shouted out **loud!**

So one day Sadie decided she had—had enough.
She started walking with a wooden **cane**.
Of course by doing so, she was just throwing more
Gossip fuel into the **flame!**

But what they didn't **know**
Was that this cane was only for **show!**

When the kids came **around**
While she was in town…
She would just give them a little poke
With the end of her cane…
And boy did they shout out **loud.**
It sure did bring on chuckles from everyone **around!**

For in the end of her **cane**
She had placed a **nail.**

Best idea Sadie had ever **had.**
She didn't care if everyone thought her **mad!**
One thing for sure…
She was never again harassed by another **lad!**

But she did live up to her name.
It was just another in a line of pranks
By the **Lady**
They called *'Crazy Sadie!!'*

…

Man Full-Pockets

Here tell…
A long time ago there was a man who was called
Man Full-Pockets!

It is said that he got this name because
when he went shopping he would fill his pockets
plumb full as he walked through the **store**.
They left him alone…
That is until he headed for the exit **door**.
At that point, he had to empty everything out onto the **floor**.
Then he was shown the **door!!**

…

Water

Most of the earth is covered by water.
Our bodies also are mostly water.
They say we should drink lots of water.
Water! Water! Water!

But you see—I have a problem with **this**
For water—I **detest!**

Perhaps 'detest' is too **strong**.
But I have been told this for so **long!**

Perhaps it isn't the water I **protest**
But rather its' importance being over **stressed!**

After reevaluating this **matter,**
I have decided not to dwell on the **latter.**

I will give it a whirl and see what develops!

I make no **promises…**
Diet Coke is my **nemesis!**

…

(From "A Smile in Rhyme)

The Awaited Letter

Everyday she waited for the mailman.
Everyday she was disappointed.
She so wanted to just receive that one envelope.
If it ever came, it would solve all her problems.

======================================

A few months **back**
From her job, she had been **sacked.**
But ambition she did not **lack!**

She didn't know what she was going to **do.**
Between her social security and her mere salary,
She was barely able to make **due.**

Now unemployed, she didn't know where to **turn.**
That is why for the mail she did so **yearn.**
When that most important envelope came…
Then and only then would her destiny be **learned!**

Then one day it **came.**
Right there in her mailbox it **laid!**

At first she was afraid to open **it…**
She didn't want to be disappointed yet again.
But upon opening it her eyes **lite**
And her mouth did smile.

Her letter was from her daughter.
She was asking her to come live with **them.**
She had hoped for this invitation,
But really wasn't sure if it would come in the **end!**

She accepted and moved in with **them...**
But only while her future was on the **mend!**
She was very thankful for the helpful hand
Her daughter was willing to **lend!**

The End!!

...

Do Not Lie to Me!

He told such **lies**.
She wasn't sure she would ever again be able to look him in the **eyes!**

First he said he was a fireman.
When she learned that was not true
He said that...
'He had said he had always wanted to be a fireman"
and **that <u>she</u> must have misunderstood.**

Then he said he was a lawyer.
But he wasn't!
Again, <u>She</u> misunderstood.
He said—he only said he roomed with a lawyer!

She was beginning to doubt her own **sanity...**
But she was sure he was the one doing all the story telling.
On his honesty she was not **depending!**

She took the day off, and she followed and **stocked!**
In the end she could not believe what she discovered...
She was in **shock!**

This man,
This man that she was falling for,
This man who she had spent many a night with...
Was employed as a dishwasher at a local bar.
He had passed the bar alright...
Just not the legal **kind.**
What was she going to do with her **find?**

She had nothing against his line of work.
But apparently he **did**.
Should she let him know that she was aware of his **fib?**

She took matters into her own hands.
She waited outside of the bar **door**
And when he came out…he was **floored!**

He started to make up another **story**…
But she told him to save it…His stories were getting **boring.**

They then went for coffee
and they talked until the sun came **up.**
Her departure was very **abrupt.**
She could not get him to shut **up!**

He was a story teller
and didn't know when to **stop.**
So she told him
That as for dates…he was the worst of the **lot!**

She left him with his mouth hanging open.
He didn't know why she was **bolting.**
Her hope was that the next person he meets
Will find out right away that
HE IS FULL OF BALONEY!!

…

The Man and His Bus Ride

I once met a man who shared with me
His experiences of taking a trip across the country…
BY **BUS!**

I really couldn't figure out why he was making such a **fuss!**

I thought, ok you get on the **bus…**
And then you get off the **bus.**
How difficult could it **be?**
The in between was the story he shared with **me!**

You are in charge of your own luggage.
You had better hope that the bathroom in the back of the bus
is clean because that is your only option
should the urge occur…and on a long ride—it **will.**
There is no time for a **meal!**
You are in charge of your own snacks and/or beverages.

The bus does not stop for anything…Not even fuel.
You do change buses along the way,
But you have to hurry from one to the **next.**
This can leave you very **perplexed!**

The man went on and on about his recent **ride.**
He said that if he had to go across country again…
He would **DRIVE!**

…

A Catholic Education

We were raised Catholic
They built a Catholic High School just as it was time to **start**.
So off I went to make my **mark!**

We wore uniforms of **brown.**
Plaid with white blouses and sweaters, pants were not **allowed!**

We were taught by nuns and **priests.**
We prayed and learned to speak with respect, honor, and to be **meek.**

The nuns were tough, they took no **guff.**
In each of us, they looked for the diamond in the **rough.**

The boys and girls were kept **separate,**
For the boys' attention, we were **desperate!**

I found Catholic high school tough as it comes.
And when I graduated, I was happy beyond **belief.**
And even though I was getting a diploma,
The scares from all those years were **deep!**

The stories that everyone tells about the Nuns using rulers to discipline students are all **true.**
But the numbers were **few!**

Catholic School Education has changed a lot over the years.
There are fewer Nuns to teach and raise **thunder.**
And the uniforms have all but gone **asunder!!**

...

(From "A Smile in Rhyme")

Babies

Babies are wonderful.
You hold them tight and give them **kisses,**
And when they sleep, our ears listen and our heart **misses!**

At first all they do is sleep and spit **up.**
As we watch them sleep,
in our throats we get this big **lump!**

We know they won't stay our little angels for **long…**
and that soon they will be grown and **gone!**

…

(From "A Smile in Rhyme)

Do Not Judge A Book by Its Cover

I once had a dilemma of **sorts**
I met a lady whose face was covered in **warts!**

I was assigned to work with her every**day,**
It was hard to concentrate and keep my curiosity at **bay!**

She didn't seem to be self-conscious at **all.**
In fact working with her was a **ball!**

We worked together for many **months,**
And after awhile I didn't even notice her **bumps!**

~~~~~~~~~~~~~~~~~

The moral of this rhyme is that
we should never judge a book by its cover.
We all already know this…
But oftentimes we forget and **stare**
or comment
on something that is non of our **affair!**

We should accept a person for who they are
not for their appearance.
This applies to a homeless person as **well.**
They can't help the hand they were **dealt.**

Their apparel may not be what you or I would **wear,**
Or not even what they would choose if they had their rathers...
But on this they can not afford to dwell.
So next time you or I are tempted to **stare—**
Let's not...
It could have been you or I out **there!!**

...

A Love Story

I would like to tell you a love story about a man I **know**
Who in his younger years…
His seeds he did **sow!**

He married and had a family,
But after a few years
He wondered why he had married…
The reason he did not **know!**

Meantime there was a young lady who
was experiencing the same **situation.**
She lived several miles away in a different **location!**

But as fate would have it she eventually moved
Back to her home **state**
Where a new life she intended to **make!**

She went to work at a public service **store**
And who do you suppose walked right through the **door?**
It was of course the young man that was mentioned **before!**

After seeing her at the counter
he made it a point to visit the **store,**
whether he needed anything or not…
He just would not be **ignored!**

After much persuasion she did indeed agree
to go out with this man…
This man who had become almost an annoyance.

It turns out that they went to high school together,
But neither remembered the other.
Soon they developed a lasting **relationship.**
One that was based on a sound **friendship!**

They did eventually **marry.**
(It wouldn't be a love story if they hadn't.)
She is so happy to have finally met a man who is so **caring!**

He agrees that it is much better the second time around
and says that if he would have known her in high **school**
you can bet she would have been at the top of his dating **pool!**

Neither regrets their past relationships.
Without them they would not be who they are today.
Nor would they have their children and beautiful grandchildren.

I do believe that they have it right this **time.**
And to watch them together, is a blessing of **mine!**

So as I bring my love story to an **end;**
I just want to say that…
"Everything Happens for a Reason"
And that is the advice I **lend!!**

…

His Spirit Was Left Behind

She hated her father…
Perhaps 'hate' is too strong of a word.

He had abused her and her sister and any other human
wearing a **skirt.**
He wasn't handsome, not even what you would call a **flirt.**

When he **passed**
She thought they were rid of him at **last.**

But one night she felt someone sitting on the edge of her **bed.**
He came to visit her more than once…
She wasn't sure when this would **end!**

She wasn't afraid of him.
She had gotten over that several years before.
But she did not want him visiting her in spirit
anymore than she wanted to visit him when he was **alive.**
He was one man who deserved to **die!**

After her mother **passed,**
She was grateful for now her visits home could stop at **last!**

She wanted to put the **past**
In the **past!**

She wanted his nightly visits to stop.
So she destroyed everything she owned that was linked to **him.**
She had read once that—that is how you get rid of **them!**

Then the next time his spirit came and sat on her bed
She told him to get out and never come **back.**
It worked…She realized that dealing
with spirits was something for which she had acquired a **knack!**

…

He Was My Father

None of us knows what we would do in a certain **situation**
until we ourselves were to face that **situation.**

However, I have trouble rationalizing why someone would
go to their father's death bed…
When while he was alive, he mistreated her so.

` ` `

I know a lady, who had been abused by her father several times,
In her bedroom he would **lurk.**
Even when he was on his death bed
He reached over and pulled up her **skirt.**

That is why I can not understand how she could go to him
when he was **ill,**
and sit with him while he went down**hill.**

I did not know this man's history until he left this world.
And that is a good thing because I would not—
Nor could I have, visited him and acted like he was a nice
normal **man.**
I would not have been able to extend a friendship **hand!**

When you ask her about it,
She simply says…"**He was my father**"!

I also know of a man who fathered two children by his very own daughter.
The children were both born with some sort of handy cap.
He suffered a very justified painful death.
He was in great pain for a long time.
On his deathbed he told his daughter—in a not so nice **manner**
That *she would always remember* her **father.**
She too sat with her father as he passed.

She did what she considered her duty!
She simply says…"**He was my father**"!

…

Tipsy

There once was a dog that was smart as a **whip**.
His owners thought so too and they hated it when they left him;
Because often times he became bored and would **whimper!**

They would put him in the laundry room when they left the **house.**
Most times he would just lie down and be quiet as a **mouse!**

One day they put him in the laundry room and went off to work.
For some reason the little fellow
was not in the mood to lie down or take a nap.
Instead he started investigating this **room.**
This room which he hoped he would get let out of **soon!**

He became VERY bored that **day.**
On his bed he chose not to **lay!**

This is where my story begins!

In the corner there was stack of cans in the **room.**
He didn't know what they were, but he did know that he
was bored and in the chewing **mood!**

He bit the first can and something came spraying out.
It sprayed on him, on the walls and on to the **floor.**
He licked it and decided he liked it and wanted **more!**

So he just kept biting into one can and then another.
Licking as much up as he could.

When his human parents came home they immediately
opened the laundry room door to let him out.
They were shocked by what happened next.

He came staggering out and could hardly walk on all fours.
He smelled of beer.
The little guy was **drunk**...
Drunk as a **Skunk!**

They investigated the laundry room and found beer all over
the **floor**
and the inside of the **door!**

They made sure their little dog got rest and kept an eye on him
all that night and the next **day.**
All he managed to do was—on his bed he **laid.**

They decided to find a new place for him to be when they
were **out.**
A place where he can watch out the window
and keep his boredom from returning.
A place he would like and not **pout!**
As for his bingeing days...
They are over; of this I have no **doubt!**

...

O.C.D.

There is this "little" thing I **do.**
It doesn't harm anyone, but me…I can assure **you!**

They even have a name for it.
It's called "Obsessive Compulsive **Disorder".**
Do I need a **Lawyer?**

I got this label because I am what some call 'a neat **freak'.**
But the outcome of that is not so **bleak!**
I simply am very—very **neat!**

The upside to **this**
is that I can manage a very long to-do **list.**
I can organize circles around others
while their panties are all in a **twist!**

The downside falls on those who have to live with **me.**
Because neat and tidy they need to **be!**

Organization and Tidiness
Is just an **extension**
Of my neatness **obsession!!**

…

(From "A Smile in Rhyme")

A Typical Boy

Once upon a time there was a young boy.
He was your 'typical boy'.
By that I mean he tried everything…
No matter how dangerous it was.

It all started when he was very young.
He stuck a metal piece from a toy into the electric outlet.
Sparks Flew, The lights went out, and
His parents came flying through the bedroom **door.**
Need I say **more!**
He was fine BECAUSE at the end of this piece of metal
there was a piece of plastic, which he just happened to be
hanging onto.
But it did knock his butt to the **floor!**

Then there was time he stuck a tin collar piece
of chimney framing over
his head and it got stuck on his neck.
The tin collar had to be cut off.

Once he decided he wanted to light a candle in his room—
and started his room on **fire.**
He went outside and got the garden hose and put
it through his bedroom window and put the fire out.
All by himself!
If I told you his parents weren't upset, I would be a **liar!**
He had to replace the window screen and clean up the mess.

He was always having accidents while riding his bike.
Running into mail boxes…curbs…etc.
Even broke his leg once.
His mother's reaction to that one is a whole other **story**!
And believe me it isn't **boring**!

When he started driving, he had an automobile accident,
and broke his **jaw**.
He ran into a brick **wall**!

His parents got their grey hairs from worrying over this **guy**.
Even though he was the apple of their eye!

Now he is grown and has children of his **own**.
God blessed him with two sons;
To which accidents, they too are **prone**.

Now it is his turn to collect his own grey **hairs**.
Especially since they always do everything in **pairs**!

And his parents…
Well they watch and grin at all the things
he says his boys **do**.
And how they are always black & **blue**!

One thing is for sure…
Parenting comes with **joys**…
And their grandsons too are typical **boys**!!

(To my handsome son, with love.)

…

The Tom Boy

There once was a little girl.
No matter how hard her parents tried,
They could not turn her into a 'girlie girl'.
It was such a battle to get her into a **dress,**
that most of the time her mother didn't even try.
She threw such **fits!**

As she grew they finally just gave up.
They accepted that their daughter was a tom boy...
A very pretty tom boy!

She ran track and played basketball.

She could and still can...
Change the oil in her car, change a tire
as well as anything electrical that needs to be done!

She can use any power **tool,**
and tackles anything and everything that there is to **do!**

She has a green thumb
And can tell you the names of all kinds of flowers
And bushes and **trees.**
How she does it, is beyond me, her Mom can only grow **weeds!**

She grew into the most wonderful woman you would every
want to **meet.**
She will drop everything to go help out someone in **need...**
Even with the smallest of **things.**

She still doesn't wear dresses.
She isn't into fashion and **lace**.
She is however into being herself.
She is a beautiful woman who grew up learning how to take care of herself.
She lives her life to the fullest.
When she is not working, she and her partner
are always doing something or going **someplace**.
The fact that she is gay…
To her family, has never brought **disgrace**.

In this family, there is no room for prejudice;
Just joy and happiness over the fact
that their daughter has grown into the wonderful person she is!

A person with the big heart full of compassion.
A friend to everyone,
A daughter to be proud of.
A daughter to love and respect.
And a daughter to envy for all she has accomplished.
Even if she still is a 'tom boy'!!

(To my daughter, with love.)

…

The Little Girl

Once upon a time there was this little girl
who wanted to be a veterinarian
when she grew up.

She loved animals of every kind…large and **small**.
She just loved them **all!**

As a child she wanted to have a **pet**,
But her father was against them all.
Let's just say his priority was paying the **rent!**

He explained to her that having a pet was a great responsibility.
There were shots and you had to get it 'fixed' so there
would be no additional pets running **around.**
She understood all this, but none the less
his explanation brought on a great big **frown!**

The first 'stray' she brought home were two kittens.
She told her mother that the lady across the **street**
Was going to have them put to **sleep**
if someone didn't take them off her hands immediately
and take them into their home to **keep!**

Well what was her mother to do?
They kept them…but they were to be kept outside.
Since they were brother and sister…
Nature took over and
soon there were more little kittens walking around.
They were beautiful kittens with long **hair.**

The little girl told her Dad that he wouldn't even know they were **there.**
There were no shots or vet visits!

But as the girl grew she was able to do the right thing with her pets.
The first pet that she chose to adopt was a guinea pig…
A beautiful white long haired guinea pig.
Well as luck would have it—it was a female and unknowingly—**pregnant.**
This called for hands-on **management!**

Then she grew to a young adult and moved out of her parents' house.
The first pet she acquired at that stage in her life was a cat.
And then another cat and another and so on.
ALL at the same **time.**
I thought she was out of her **mind!**

She also loved dogs and had her share of those as **well.**
She even owned a horse once, but with a horse there is that **SMELL!**

Her reputation spread and people dropped their stray cats off at her **door.**
She couldn't add any**more**
to what she already had inside her home.
So she collected them, took them to the vet, had them 'fixed' and got them their shots…
And then she found homes for them or kept them outside.
If she would have taken anymore inside, there would have been **war!**

She never did become a **vet,**
She really should have though.
If she had it to do over again…
Her being a **vet,**
is the occupation on which I would have **bet!!**

…

The Wondering Boy

A long time ago there was a young boy
Who just wanted to play and **play**…
That is all he wanted to do all **day!**

His parents told him that he also had to do **chores.**
Well he did not want to do chores of **course!**

So one day he ran **away.**
Just packed up his favorite toy and off he went.
From home his parents didn't think he would really **stray!**

But off he **went.**
He wondered into the forest behind his **house.**
He became **lost**—
And then he **wept!**

He must have fallen asleep because when he **woke**
He realized that the sun had gone away and
He couldn't see anything and then he fell
And hurt his leg…fearing it may be **broke!**

Then all of a sudden he was surrounded by animals…
Small Friendly Animals!

They talked to him and he understood every word they said.
They asked him for his **story**—
and as he talked they listened very attentively
because they thought his story not **boring.**
When he was finished they told him they understood his situation
But that no matter who you are; animal or human—

There are certain responsibilities that you must perform
Or the whole order of things could not keep on **going!**

They explained to him how even the lowly worm or **ant**
plays a major role in how its community **acts!**

They told him that he must be on his **way,**
And that from his home he should not **stray!**

They all agreed that it was too late for him to start **out,**
And so they stayed with him until the sun came **out!**
And then they heard them…
His family calling out for him in loud **shouts!**

He started crying and they heard him calling back to **them.**
And soon they were all reunited **again!**

He told his parents about his animal friends,
And they smiled at each other…
Not wanting to doubt him!

He told his parents that he was sorry for worrying **them.**
He told them that from now on he would do his chores,
Without them asking **him!**
They hugged and kissed **him…**
And there was no scolding.

They did however ask him what kind of punishment they
should give him.
After all he had scared them to **death**
when he **left!**

He thought and **thought**—
And then he said that he guessed he shouldn't be allowed to
watch TV or play any video games for a **month**.
He figured that much punishment **ought**
to be **enough!**

Well his parents were just so happy to find him alive
they told him that they too thought that was a fair
punishment.
However, his thinking of it was **enough,**
and on him they weren't planning on being so **tough!**

He promised to do as he was **told.**
He promised to do his chores without being **told.**
And he promised never again to leave home…
At least not until he was very—very **old!!**

…

The Temper

He had a temper…
A temper that he did not like to **show**.
Somehow he managed to keep it under **control**…
until with his family he was **alone!**

This was not a good thing.
You see, he liked to hit **things**.
Things like other human **beings!**

His wife took the brunt of most of **it**.
But sometimes when he was having a **fit**,
He would take it out on whoever was close by…
And the children would be the ones he chose to **hit!**

He was a well known professional in his **community**.
No one would ever have thought this of him.
His wife never fought for her **liberty!**

She should have taken the children and **left**,
But she knew that he would bring her back…
On that she was willing to **bet!**

And who would have believed her **anyway**…
For the children's' sake, she knew she needed to get **away!**

He knew how to abuse them without leaving a visible **mark**.
And after one of his fits, he was always happy as a **lark!**

He blamed them of course.
He would tell them that it was all their fault.

Then one day he had—had a very bad day at work.
The market was down and his clients were having a **fit**.
So on his way home he stopped off for a drink or two…
Just to give his spirits a **lift!**

He was late getting home and his wife already had the children fed.
He was furious, and thought she should have waited on him.
He started throwing the dishes onto the **floor,**
And was shouting in a loud **roar!**

Next he of course reached for her,
And started to hit her and verbally abuse her.

She fell to the **floor…**
He wouldn't be able to abuse her **anymore.**
He had gone too far this time.
She hit her head on the table as she fell to the **floor.**
He didn't know what to do…so he ran out the back **door!**

The children called the police,
And the neighbors gathered **around.**
Sympathy for the children was **abound!**

The father!!!
Well they found him.
He was picked up for drunken driving.
When calling it in the officer discovered
That his driving was not all he was involved in.

Today the children are living with their grandparents.
They adjusted well and seem happy **enough**.
Of course their mother, they miss very **much**!

The mother's prayers were answered…
her children are safe.
Safe from their father's abuse.
Safe from the physical and mental **pain**.
And she looks down on them each and every **day**!

The children!!!
They are happy their father got sent **away**.
They know that for their freedom,
it was a big price their mother **paid**!!

…

…

My husband said that was a 'way to dark'

Rhyme…so hopefully the next one will

get us back on the lighter side!!

…

The Word "Awfully"

Let's examine the word *awful* and *awfully.*

We say…"He had an awful fate."

Then we say…"It was awfully good."

The dictionary defines 'awful' as…
"inspiring awe…terrifying…very bad"

'Awfully' is defined as…
"in an awful way…very awful"

Is it just me, or does the above make no sense at all?

~~~~~~~~~~~~~~~~~~~~~~

I only bring this subject up because it is something that bothers the heck out of my husband.
So I thought why not look into **it.**
I thought perhaps this light bulb in my head might become **lit!**

Well no light bulbs went off,
I may have gotten a new wrinkle in my brain from learning this though.

I have often wondered where and who decided on
What words we use and how they are **spelled.**
Researching this is something for which I am **compelled!**

Another time, another **day**.
For now I will let it **lay!**

So as I come to end of my rhyme…
I hope you have an 'awfully nice day'
And that nothing 'awful' happens between now and **then.**
These are the thoughts I have to **lend!!**

…

BUNS

Today's grocery shopping **trip**
was just like any other **trip**.

It wasn't her favorite thing to **do,**
But she did it and bought things for which the price she **knew!**

She picked up this and **that**…
Including items that would make a good **snack!**

When she arrived at the check out counter
she placed her items on the conveyer belt **fast.**
(They were busy and she didn't want to hold up the line!)
Non crushable items first…
Saving the breakable and crushable until **last.**

The last item she placed was a package of hamburger buns.
She thought nothing of this until a man behind her in line
Told her she had *'nice buns'.*
She patted them and said *"Yes they are…very soft buns!"*

Well the man started laughing and gave her a look,
She "GOT IT" at last!

She turned to him and he said "I couldn't help myself."
And he laughed **again.**
She simple said that's ok!
And that was all the communication she had with **him!**
Although she did think that him saying that, he was putting
himself out there on that 'sexual **limb'.**

When she thinks back on it all now she refers to her back exterior as *'The Famous Buns"...*
After all, it was done in FUN!!

...

The Flushing Toilet

There once was a couple who welcomed into their home
two young girls from **Japan.**
Their names, I do not have on **hand!**

They were with a church **group.**
They didn't speak much English.
And it was hard getting them into the American **loop!**

On their first night at the couple's home
The couple was awakened by giggles and snickers.
The girls were amazed by the *'flushing'* toilet.
So consequently they were repeatedly flushing it.
The couple didn't do anything; they consider it a learning experience!

The girls flushed the toilet and ran water in the **tub.**
They were from a very backward family,
and thought this great **fun.**
The next morning at breakfast,
The subject was not brought up.
The couple was just happy that the
Giggles, Snickers, and Running Water were **done!**

...

The Little Girl Who Decorated

There once was a little girl.
She was like all children—in that she was inquisitive.

She had watched her mother around the house,
painting and putting up wallpaper.

One night they had invited their minister over for supper.
Dinner went well.
The children had behaved.

After dinner the minister had asked to use the restroom.
They directed him and when he returned they sat down,
had coffee and dessert.
Nothing unusual was discussed and they bid him farewell on
a good note.

After putting the children to bed and cleaning up the kitchen,
the hostess herself went to use the restroom before turning in.
Words could not describe her shock at what she discovered.

The walls in the bathroom were covered with sanitary napkins!!

Apparently their daughter had decided *'to decorate'*.
She peeled off the stick strip and went to it.
They knew it was her because she could only reach up so far.

The mother was beyond embarrassment…
What must the minister have thought when he used the restroom?

The subject was never brought **up**...
Not to the little girl or the minister.
She just couldn't handle the **embarrassment!!**

...

Green Thumb

A Green Thumb is something I never had, not really.
I grew my gardens inside with Miracle Grow by my **side**.
They grew and grew and when asked what my trick was…I **lied!**

I didn't know one flower or tree from **another.**
I only knew which one I liked better than the **other!**

Now my mother was the expert and whatever she planted **grew.**
We had flowers and vegetables **too.**

She canned what she could and we ate very **well,**
while outside the snow **fell!**

I know that talent is handed on down.
What I don't know is if it can skip a generation on its way down.
But that must **be…**
For my daughter can plant and grown rings around **me!!**

…

(From "A Smile in Rhyme")

The Monkey Bars

There was a young boy,
Who while on a picnic with his family and relatives
Got his head stuck in the monkey bars.

No one had ever thought that his head was particularly large.
But there he was—**STUCK!**
What bad **luck!**

They all tried to free him from being **stuck,**
But they had No **Luck!**

They had to call the fire department…
To get him un-**stuck.**
This boy with the bad **luck.**
They all saw it when it pulled up…
That Big Red Fire **Truck!**

By now the young boy was crying and could not be comforted.
Not by his mother, grandmother or even the firemen.
He was embarrassed and just wanted to be **free.**
The firemen told everyone to **leave…**
One fireman said "Leave this to **me**"!

Soon the boy was **free**
And the fire truck did **leave.**
The little boy looked at all the people standing around
and said…"All this was For **Me?**"

Well from that point on the young boy no longer played on monkey bars.
He was worried about his bad **luck**...
His bad luck at again getting **stuck!**

...

She couldn't help herself!

She couldn't help **herself.**
If she didn't eat all the ice cream right now—it would **melt!**

She couldn't help **herself.**
They were fresh out of the oven.
She ate one roll and then another…
She knew they were best warm.
If she didn't eat them all right now—the frosting would **melt!**

She couldn't help **herself.**
They were just laying there on the cookie sheet…
Waiting to cool and have someone eat one of them.
She helped herself and couldn't stop at the first one.
Before she knew it, she had eaten every cookie
on that cookie sheet.
If she didn't eat them all right now—they would get hard,
and they were better warm and soft…that is how she **felt!**

She couldn't help **herself.**
It was the cutest pair of blue jeans she had every seen.
She tried them on and discovered she could barely see her knees.
The jeans looked better on the display.
If she hadn't eaten all the ice cream,
the rolls, and the cookies…
Right Now—She would be able to wear those cute jeans…
*That is how she **felt!!***

…

Fingers

The other day I was asked how many fingers does Homer Simpson have.
Well I figured it was a trick question so I did **hesitate**.
Cartoons often times do **exaggerate!**

Of course I knew to whom she was referring,
But I had never seen **Homer;**
Nor did I understand his **humor!**

I pondered this for a few minutes and then I spit it out.
I said I did not know, ***BUT***
Since it seems he is supposed to be life like—
I would have to say **eight!**
I must have answered correctly
because my friend didn't have a come back…
She just said my answer was **great!**

I am guessing she thought I would include his thumbs and answer ten!
A lot of people make that mistake!

So what is this rhyme about, you ask?

Nothing really,
Just that the next time someone says to count on your fingers,
Or hold out your fingers…
Surprise them and hold back the thumbs!!

…

Social Security

On a more serious **note**…
Let's see if this subject will **float your boat!**

The baby boomers of this time in **history**
Worry about their social **security.**

Retirement sometimes has to be put off
due to the high cost of **living.**
They say there isn't going to be anything for us…
But yet we are supposed to keep on **contributing!**

We place the blame here and **there**…
But our comments go right up into the **air!**

It is certainly a problem…no denying **that.**
It will be more of worry to our children and on down…
AND THAT IS A **FACT!!!**

…

The Weekend Vacation

There once was this lady who took a weekend **vacation**.
She, her husband, and grown daughter shared a room at
their chosen motel **location.**

During the night the lady had to use the bathroom.
Being considerate, she waited until the door was closed
to turn on the light.
In her attempt to reach the switch, she backed up too **far**
And into the bathtub she fell with a **start!**

So there she sat with legs over the **side**
And the shower curtain under her **backside!**

After the initial shock wore off, she tried to get up.
She was careful for she didn't want the shower curtain
to come down on her **head.**
But each time she tried, back into the bathtub she fell…like **lead!**

She then got to laughing so hard, her husband she **woke.**
He came in to assist, but upon seeing the sight
He too out into laughter **broke!**

They laughed as quietly as they **could.**
Their daughter was asleep on the other side of the wall,
Or so they under**stood!**

Once rescued and composed, they returned to **bed**.
A response from their daughter…
"I hope you two were having fun in there!"
Set them to laughing once **again!!**

…

(From "A Smile in Rhyme")

Just Believe

I **See**
You **See**
&
We **Believe!!**

We also believe in what we can't **see**.
And we believe in what is beyond our ability to **see**.

Just because you can't SEE something, doesn't mean it isn't **there**.
We can't see God…
But we can see Him in everything around us,
In ourselves and even in the **air!**

We can't see God,
But we can see his works!

Some people say things like;
He doesn't answer me!
Or I haven't seen any miracles!

I say—
Yes he does and Yes you have!!

All you have to do is ask Him
and
Listen!

I **See**
You **See**
&
We **Believe!!**

...

The Baby Brother

Once upon a time there was a little girl who very much wanted a baby brother.
She presented this to her parents and was told that they would think about **it**.
Of course this was a **fib**!

She asked them where to go to get a baby.
They told her that babies were 'gotten' in two different ways…
One was that they were delivered by giant **storks**.
This gave the little girl a fright of **sorts**.

The other was that they were found in cabbage patches.
You opened up the cabbage like a **lid**.
Of course this was also a **fib**!

She wasn't really satisfied with these answers
so one day she asked her grandmother where babies came from.
Her grandmother looked her right in the **eye**
and told her that when a mommy and daddy wanted a baby,
they prayed really hard and if their prayers were answered,
they would be 'given' a baby.
Of course this too was a **fib**
Sort of a white **lie!**

She liked this answer better than the **previous**
and she decided to be very **devious!**

She thought that if her mommy and daddy wanted a baby
'as she had hopped they did', which would be so **dandy**.
Then she would help them out by including in her nightly prayers
a request for a new baby for her **family**.

She didn't tell her parents about her prayers,
She just prayed and prayed with all her **might**
Each and every **night!**

It seemed like it took forever, but one day she realized
her prayers had been answered.
She overheard her mommy talking to daddy
and mommy said that she was going to have a baby,
and she had just learned that it was a **boy.**
She saw that her daddy could not contain his **joy!**

She ran into the room and jumped onto her mommy's **lap.**
And as she did so, she began to **laugh!**

SHE BEEMED!!

Her parents were not quite sure what was going on with their little girl.
They told her their news and her reply was, "I know!"...
"I just want to know why it took so long?"

The parents looked at each other and smiled.
The little girl smiled as well.
Only her smile was directed up to God
Who she knew had answered her prayers.

And that she knew was not a Lie or Fib!!!

...

The Squirrel

A lady went out into her yard,
The reason I don't remember.
She frightened a squirrel half to **death**
And up her skirt he **fled!**

He ran up one leg, across her middle
and down the other leg trying to escape!

Needless to say this all happened in just a matter of seconds,
And left the lady in pure exasperation!

Her husband was watching from the window **inside**
and to her aid, he had not **time!**

He laughed, but she only **frowned.**
It took her awhile to settle **down!**

When this story is told, it is received with **doubt.**
It sounds like something out of a story tellers' **mouth.**

But I can assure you that it is **true,**
I wouldn't lie to **you!**

...

(From "A Smile in Rhyme")

The Country Mouse

We all know the story about the country mouse and city mouse.
But I'll bet you haven't heard it as told below:

+++

There once was a country mouse
that lived in the state of Alabama.
He lived on a **farm**,
In a big red **barn**.

He worked each and every **day**…
He worked hard for his **pay**.
In the **hay** he did not **lay!**

This particular mouse had a **talent**…
a very special **talent!**

He could play the banjo with his **feet;**
But getting him to do it was hard because he was so **meek.**
He did all this while standing on his head
And he was also playing the harmonica at the same time.
He enjoyed his music very much.
But just thinking of performing in front of anyone
Made his knees **weak!**

He performed when he was alone.
The other occupants of the **barn**
and **farm**
sometimes could hear him and not to
disturb him they became quiet as a mouse!
(No pun intended.)

But it wasn't enough for the little country **mouse**.
He wanted more…more than just living in his little barn **house!**

He called up his cousin in the city of **Mobridge**.
He told him that he was ready to cross over the BIG **bridge**
to come see him.

Well off he went…banjo and harmonica in **hand**.
He wasn't sure what he would find in this distant **land!**

First he had to cross over the BIG bridge.
He was afraid he would fall between the boards.
He kept close to the sides so if he were to start to **fall**
He would be able to grab onto something.
And if he did **fall,**
he figured he could survive if he rolled up into a round **ball!**
(After all, he was known for his flexibility.)

The trip was long and **lonely**.
He questioned his decision to leave the red barn.
After all, it was nice and **cozy!**

One night a big storm **came.**
The rain forced him to be **delayed!**

He was cold and **damp,**
And he had no more food left in his back **pack!**

He was a little afraid **too.**
He wasn't sure what he should **do!**

The next morning he dumped the water out of his shoes.
He put them in the sun to **dry,**
And he lay on a branch up **high…**
He studied the **sky!**

He saw clouds that reminded him of the barn animals
and friends that he had left behind.
The more he looked up to the **sky,**
The more he wondered **why…**
Why had he left home.
The home that he could see in his mind's **eye!**

He decided to return **home.**
He was tired of being **alone.**
Alone on that long journey **road!**

Again he faced the problem
of having to cross over that scary bridge.
But he came up with a solution.
He put his banjo in the river that ran under the bridge…
and he jumped inside the banjo.
He floated on down the river…
Laid back and played his harmonica.
He played it as loud as he could.
He had no one **around**
until he would land on **ground!**

He finally returned home…
Back home to that Big Red **Barn.**
He was met with kisses and **arms…**
A lot of **arms!**

Everyone was so happy to see he had returned.
That night they had a party.
A party that was attended by all.
And the little mouse played his banjo and harmonica.
He played as loud as he could.
He was so glad to be home.
He forgot all about the meekness he had for crowds.
There was dancing and eating…fun was had by all.
//
//

The moral of this story
(hopefully you can see one)
Is that the grass isn't always greener on the other side of the fence.
It just looks that way because you are looking at it from a side view.
Look at it straight down and it all looks the same.

Appreciate what you have!!

…

The Pumpkin Patch

The Pumpkin Patch is a really fun **place.**
You take your child just to see the smile on their **face!**

Fun is had by **all.**
It takes place every **fall!**

A parent walks with their **child**
looking for that *perfect pumpkin,* mile after **mile.**
They walk and walk and finally the child goes **wild...**
They have found *'The Great Pumpkin'* and they **smile!**

But of course the pumpkin is too heavy for the child to **carry.**
The parent mustn't **tarry!**

Now they start their journey back.
The parent carrying the child all the way back!
A child and a pumpkin you ask!
Why yes, for love this parent did not **lack!**

There is a surprise waiting for the parent at the end of this **journey.**
Upon arriving at their destination, the child gets the **yearning**
to check out another pumpkin patch.

You guessed it, a pumpkin replacement was **found.**
What could the parent say;
the happiness coming from this child was all **around.**

The parent had to **admit**
it was a beautiful pumpkin, the best of the **pick!!**

...

(From "A Smile in Rhyme")

Gay or Straight?

Once there was a young man who was smart as a whip.
He didn't have to study as hard as some,
And he always received the highest grade.

He wasn't really into **sports,**
But at the persistence of his parents—
He played them of **course!**

He dated some, but that wasn't really his **thing.**
He did it mostly to fit in with his peers…
That sort of **thing!**

He went on to attend college.
He dated a young lady and they even moved in together.
But that didn't last **long.**
He said it was because they argued a lot and she was always **wrong!**

He is a grown man now.
And he still lives **alone.**
The reason probably will never be **known!**

Some thought that perhaps he is **gay.**
Some thought that perhaps he just can't find the right **mate!**

It is sad really because whatever the reason;
Life is much more fulfilling with a **mate.**
It is never too **late!**

So I say to this young man…
Gay or Straight—
Get out there and find you a Mate!!

...

Sweet Girl

Once upon a time there was a little **girl**.
She was pretty much like every other **girl**.
Except for one thing…
She was the youngest of three AND the only **girl!**

As in all families, the youngest child gets more **attention**.
Well that plus the fact that she was a little girl—A fact I did **mention**.

This child could not have been **sweeter,**
You would just have to of met **her!**

She was smart as a **whip**.
And I never heard her give her parents any **lip!**

She was very lucky because when she wasn't in Pre-School
She got to go to work with both her Mommy and her **Daddy**.
She knew the office rules, and her behavior was just **dandy!!**

…

The Little Puppy

She was lost and unwanted, but now she has been **found**…
She is now forever **bound**
To the family with plenty of love all **around!**

She was used by a puppy **mill,**
to reproduce at their **will**.

When at last they were dissatisfied
Or finished with this little **angel,**
Off to the pound they sent her, with her fate in **peril!**

She watched for a familiar **face,**
But there were none in this **place!**

One day a lady came in and wanted to see this cute little dog.
The lady said the dog was just what she had been hoping **for,**
She took her home and the little dog was alone no **more.**
She even has her own bed on the **floor.**
But prefers to sleep in the big bed with her new found family
who she just **adores!**

This is a match made in heaven.
The little dog no longer has to be a puppy machine…
to that they all **agree.**
All that is required of her at her new home,
Is for her to be as happy as she can possibly **be!!**

…

The Donkey

Once upon a time there was a donkey.
He was the cutest donkey you have ever **seen.**
Believe **me!**

There was only one thing wrong with **him.**
He had buck teeth that you could see even when he **grinned!**

He was very self conscious of **this.**
It even made him talk with a **lisp!**

He decided that he should go have his teeth looked **at.**
He wanted to fix these teeth
so that the other donkeys would no longer **laugh!**

Off he went and when he came back from the orthodontist
he had braces on his teeth…
Not just any old braces—he had chosen the color blue
for the wires on his **braces.**
You should have seen the other donkey's **faces!**

He became so popular among the other donkeys.
They all wanted braces…even those who didn't need them.

Every time the donkey went for his check up
He came back with a different color of wire on his braces.
They would all gather around to **see…**
The attention—he could not **believe!**

After about a year—the braces came off.
He wasn't sure if he was ready for **that.**

He was afraid that without the braces,
That the other donkeys would once again **laugh!**
After all he liked all the attention he had gotten from having them.
But he soon learned that there was another advantage
Of getting them off—
He had the nicest—brightest teeth of all the other donkeys.
Now he had the problem of fighting off all the girl donkeys.
He decided that this problem…
Was something he could live with!!

…

Religion
How can you not believe?

I have talked about this subject in prior books…
Therefore I feel it only right to include it in this one.

No matter what you believe,
We all believe that there is a greater power than us.
It doesn't matter what you call Him.
In the end there is only one…
And I call him God!

To not believe in a higher power
is just plain ignorant!

How can you not believe—
When you look around you at the flowers & trees?

How can you not believe—
When you look into a new born's face?

How can you not believe—
When you see His works in others?

How can you not believe—
*When some things happen and you know
that they were meant to be?*

How can you not believe—
When you look at the workings of the human body?

How can you not believe—
When you pray and you feel a connection to God?

To Not Believe...
Now that is a scary thought!!

...

Take it Away Please!

What is it he **thought**…
When into my house this little furry thing they just **brought**!

Is it a rabbit, no that cannot **be**.
My master wouldn't allow such a thing
into our space; this thing that does nothing but **pee**.
When is it going to **leave?**

When is it going to leave,
this little pee-wee thing?

I think it must be here to **stay**
Because on my master's lap it does **lay!**
*Please, please take it **away!***

I was here first, my master belongs to **me**.
*Oh please, please make it **leave**.*

I have pouted and ignored my family.
I have been having a tantrum **fit**.
*Please, please, just take **it!***

I have laid and watched the goings on.
"Oh isn't he cute", they all **say**.
*Please, please take it **away!***

It is kind of cute, it's a little puppy baby **boy**.
I need to rethink all this, not for my sake
but for the new bundle of **joy!**

I could be his mentor, the father I was meant to **be**.
I could teach him where to **pee**.
And that will be a job, believe you **me!**
I could teach him to bark at rabbits and protect our property.
Maybe, he doesn't have to leave!!

...

(From "A Smile in Rhyme")

He Had a Knack

It was Halloween a few years **back**…
and as for decorating he had a **knack!**

He had displayed a scarecrow on his porch.
It looked really life **like,**
and even had on it, a bright **light!**

Well when Halloween **arrived**
he replaced his stuffed scarecrow with himself.
When the kids came up on the porch and
the scarecrow started talking;
Some would start to **cry.**
Others laughed so hard, they thought they would **die!**

It wasn't long before the neighborhood children
learned to expect *something* from their neighbor.
But they were never sure just what from
this neighbor who for decorating had a **knack.**
And as for creativity, his talents did not **lack!**

One Halloween he hid in the bed of his pick up truck.
He covered himself with leaves and when the
children walked **by**—
Well, he jumped up and scared them to death.
Some of them screamed with a **cry;**
Others just looked up and walked right on **by!**

Then there was the time he wore the 'mask of death'
to the door when giving out **candy.**
That wasn't too bad;
In the end we had a lot of left over **candy!**

He has mellowed in his old **age**.
I guess it was just a **phase**!

But you have to admit that this neighbor
'really' had for decorating—a **knack**.
And for fun…he did not **lack**!!

…

On A Dare

He took it on a **dare.**
All his friends were standing **there!**

It was late and very dark **out.**
They all agreed to find a garden to stake **out!**

They were up to no **good.**
He knew he would get into trouble
and at home in bed is where he **should**
be!

But he went along as they agreed to sneak into the garden.
Their plan was to pick a pumpkin or two
and then they would smash it in the **street.**
But the outlook became **bleak**
when the owner of the garden turned on the porch **light.**
He wondered, what now would be their **plight?**

They all grabbed a round pumpkin and off they ran.
When they got far enough away,
they examined the fruits of the labor.
(so to speak)
They wanted to see what they had **stolen**
from the garden of their **neighbor!**

They all had a pumpkin…That is all but one.
They all looked at what he was holding.
It was not orange…
In fact it was **green.**
Leaves as Green as they could **be!**

You see in his haste and guilt,
He grabbed whatever he could so he could just **leave**.
What he had grabbed was a large 'head of cabbage'.
Well he was as embarrassed as he could **be**.
He thought "Oh no, now they will all make fun of **me!**"

They just shook their heads and went about their business
of smashing their stolen goods into the **street**.
But as for the cabbage, its future was **bleak**.

The young boy just threw it **away**.
He vowed to never again be led **astray!**

Boys will be Boys
That we can not **deny**.
Let's just hope that in his vow, he did not **lie!!**

...

The Circle of Life

They had their click just like everyone else does when they
were in high school.
They hung out together almost every weekend.
Friends forever is where they all thought their friendship
would end!

But their click wasn't any different from other clicks and friends.
They lost track of each other after graduation.
They got busy with their own lives,
Their own families,
Careers, etc.

But as life does, it comes around…
Makes a complete circle of life, so to speak.

This is also true of ones' life as the parent who
gets involved in activities and clubs whether
it be school or church.
The young parents get involved and then when their
children out of school, the duties go on to the next
group of young parents.
A continuous circle.

In a manner of speaking the same is true for school friends.
Once you have raised your family,
retired from your job,
and finally have more time on your hands,
your mind goes to wondering what ever happened
to so-in-so.

I am not saying that nobody ever stays in touch,
But I would wager that most don't.
Our society is too big and too busy.

Also, the older we get,
The more important family and friends get.

So what am I getting at?
Simply, "The Circle of Life"!

...

To Tell You Otherwise Would be a Lie!

He was the cutest little **thing.**
He had blond hair and blue eyes;
He just melted your heart with his very **being!**

He was all boy.
By that I mean he was adventurous,
tough as nails, and he copied everything his Dad **did.**
To tell you otherwise, would be a **fib!**

Sometimes it was just too much for his Mom to take in.
When she told her mother-in-law about his antics,
she would laugh and tell her daughter-in-law
that he was just doing everything his Dad **did.**
She said to tell you otherwise, would be a **fib!**

My son used to do the very same things as your **child.**
He just ran **wild!**

He climbed doorframes and cabinets.
He would jump off things, without a worry of the **outcome.**
His head had many a **lump!**

He often held his breath until his face turned **blue**.
He survived, and so your son will **too**.
Just relax and remember that someday
He too will be a daddy and then it will be his turn **to**
Come to **you!**

To tell you otherwise, would be a lie!!

...

A Daddy for Christmas

He wanted a daddy for **Christmas.**
He put an ad in the local paper,
without his mother's knowledge.
Oh, the result turned into a royal **mess!**

Single men started coming to their **door,**
and e-mails were coming in **galore!**

When his mother figured out what was going **on,**
Her son was grounded to the great **beyond!**

She knew his heart was in the right **place,**
But advertising for a daddy was a huge **mistake!**

When she had—had all she could take
She decided to leave home until the whole thing blew **over.**
She took her son to her **mother's!**

She changed her e-mail password.
She cancelled the ad in the paper.
And she went on a trip to relax and forget her
predicament!

She had a VERY nice time.
So much so, she hated to come **back.**
But she couldn't stay longer.
Because at this point, it was funds she did **lack!**

She picked up her son and home they **went.**
She told him about this nice man that she had **met!**

Her son was so excited; he wanted to know all the **details**.
She showed him pictures and listened to his happy **wails!**

She told him that she owed him a thank you.
Because if he hadn't ran that ad she would never have taken
her trip and then she would never have met this very nice **man**.
This man who she thought was just **grand!**

The man that the lady had met on **vacation**
was actually running away from his own **situation!**

It seems his sister had put him on a dating **site**
and he was trying to forgive her with all his **might!**

He had went on a couple of blind **dates,**
but none led to his meeting his **mate!**

It turned out that he was actually from the same **town.**
The two of them decided that for a mate,
they no longer needed to look **around!**

They were happy and soon they **married.**
Their love was so strong
that where marriage was concerned,
they did not **tarry!**

If you ask the son he will tell you that his ad did the **trick**.
If you ask the mother, she will tell you that now looking back
she doesn't care a **bit**.

All that counts is that on Christmas Eve
He got a new daddy just in the nick of **time.**
And that my friends is the end of my **Rhyme!!**

...

Clouds

As an adult I saw a cloud that looked just like a **feather**.
I was lying on the ground on a blanket
and I was wearing my favorite red **sweater!**

Before the time of video games and **software,**
there was more time for looking at the clouds, way up **there!**

We would lie on the grass for hours and look up to **see**
dogs, cats, flowers and even dinosaurs, up there in that blue **sea!**

Today the clouds are still **there,**
waiting in anticipation for someone to notice their **flare!**

But children are too busy with this and **that.**
It's a shame really, to waste such beauty as **that!!**

...

His Faith!

I met a man the other **day**
who told me that although everyday he did **pray,**
entering a church was not his **way!**

I pondered this for a few minutes.
Then I asked him if he wouldn't mind giving
me an explanation for his frame of **mind…**
It was so different from **mine!**

The man told me that he used to go all the time.
He went during the week and on Sunday **too.**
But then he said he stopped going…
Just out of the **blue!**

He said that he believes that you don't have to **be**
in a church to honor God and to show how much you **believe.**

He felt that some of the people in church
shouldn't really be **there.**
God knows which ones they are,
and for those, He does **despair!**

He called them Sunday morning Christians.
The grace they showed inside the **church**
leaves them the minute they step outside.
They commit acts against God and man…
He felt that there are a lot of hypocrites in **church.**
He said one day he just stopped going to **church.**

He said he goes to church on Christmas and Easter,
but that is all.

He believes that you show your faith by actions,
and your own personal connection with **God**.
He said he talks to God each and every day.
He reads his bible daily,
and he believes his religion is between him and **God!**

I thought about what he said.

I told him although I agreed with him in that
there are a lot of people who go to church
who are more sinner that Christian;
that we can only hope that a 'little' of what they heard
will stick with them when they leave God's house.
And if it doesn't,
Well then we just have to add them to our prayer **list**.
With that he started to raise his **fist**.

At first I was frightened at what he was going to do.
But he simply raised it and agreed with me.
He said that I was a good Christian person to give them
the benefit of the doubt.
but he himself could not!

I sat there by myself for sometime after he left.
I wondered if he would ever change his mind
about going back into a church.

But if he did or didn't,
I knew he was a good Christian man…
A man who had just fallen **astray.**
And I felt that one **day**
he too would go through God's Golden Gates!!

…

Leaves

There is nothing more beautiful than the leaves in the **fall**.
Their array of colors amazing **all!**

They do have one downfall **though,**
And that is the raking required to make your yard **glow!**

They are fun to play **in…**
But then the raking will begin all over **again!**

You rake them up and put them into bags.
Then you haul them off to the dump where it cost you
Two Dollars for the each bag!

If you live outside the city limits you can burn them.
But that only leads to a fine for air pollution.
It is really cool the way they **sound**
when you go walking **around.**

And driving down a road covered in **leaves,**
They fly out of the way as if they were trying to **flee!**

The beauty of this act of **nature**
You cannot **measure!!**

…

The Frightened Puppy

There once was a **puppy**
who was as cute as he could **be!**

However he was afraid of sounds like lightening.
He would run under the bed and tremor and **shake.**
At night he kept everyone **awake!**

One day his owner brought into the house
This large box and what was in it was used to freshen the **house.**
They didn't know that it wasn't going to be quiet as a **mouse!**

Every time it started up, it snapped
and scared the puppy once again.
The owners didn't know what to **do,**
they wanted clean air and a happy puppy **too!**

One day the puppy decided he had had **enough,**
and a protest he did **conduct!**

He pouted and pouted for a whole day and a **half.**
He wouldn't even get onto his owner's **lap!**

Finally he gave in for a pat and a scratch
which was what he **needed.**
And his owner finally **conceded…**
That a new much quieter air machine was what was **needed!!**

…

(From "A Smile in Rhyme")

Dogs and Cats

I would like to rescue every stray **animal**.
All dogs and cats, but that would not be **tangible**.

It's not the animal's fault that their original owner
did not care or know enough to have them **FIXED;
OR IS IT!!!**

When babies came, it was such disorder.
Some were given away, some abandoned…
Others just discarded!

We see animals of all ages cast aside.
It could be their owner thought they were just
Too Much Trouble…
When really it's **simply**
a matter of not living up to their **responsibility!**

It breaks my heart to see a **stray**
that has been thrown **away!**

My only hope is that maybe someday
all the irresponsible pet owners will get their just rewards!!

…

I have tried many hobbies up to this point in my **life**.
I have tried whatever was popular at the moment,
no matter how **trite!**

It all started when my mother taught me how to **embroidery**.
From there I went to needlepoint;
The results were **extraordinary!**

I have free-hand painted on fabric, I enjoyed that a lot.

I painted wooden Christmas Free Decoration.
They hung by little green and red ribbons…
My favorite they were not!

My tension release is to wallpaper and **redecorate**.
I have been told that I have a talent for that.
And everything always looked **great!**

I learned to wallpaper from watching my mother.

She even did the ceilings…
I can't imagine trying to do that!

I like planning and baking for parties,
even if they aren't **mine**.
Now I am trying my hand at writing **rhyme**.
Since I have gotten older,
I'm not able to do all the other things I used to do in my **prime!**

…

The Truth...
Can you handle the truth?

Why is it that often times people will tell you
'what they **think** you want to hear...rather than telling you the truth?'

It is kind of like when a wife says to her husband...
"Do I look fat in these pants?"

Should he say, "Oh you look great honey!"
And then she goes out in public and gets laughed at behind her back!
OR
Should he simply say...
"I have seen other pants that make you look slimmer."

Another example could be that you are telling a co-worker about your personal life and all your problems.
You ask the co-worker what you should do.
The co-worker may very well
want to tell you to take your problems elsewhere...
But instead they **will agree with how they think you want them to answer.**

People, these untrue comments are not helping anyone!

I believe these types of questions should be answered with tack.
It is not what you say...but rather how you phrase it or say it!!

Some people don't want to hear the truth,
But later they will be glad someone told it to them.

It might even get to the point where they will say…
I am going to ask so-in-so, because I know they will tell me the truth!

Of course this is only my opinion of things.
You don't have to agree with me.
And if we ever meet,
you can tell me what you think.

…

Puppies Get Sick Too

Did you know that our dogs can catch
pretty much whatever we humans catch?

We don't really think about it when we have a cold, etc.
We shouldn't sneeze on them or let them lick our face
when we are not feeling well.

They know when we aren't feeling well.
That is when they decide to be **right in our face.**

Our four legged friends get diabetes, cancer, kidney failure,
and many of our other human elements.

I am telling you this because recently I have witnessed
several occasions when my dog has had indigestion problems.
I take an anti-acid everyday…
I guess maybe she should too.

When I had shoulder surgery,
Where did she want to lie????
You guessed it, right on top of the sore shoulder!

The expression "Dog is Man's Best Friend"…
Well I truly believe it!

Let's do our best to keep them safe;
Warm in the winter,
Cool in the summer.
And love them like crazy!!!

…

Last Minute Shopping

It was almost Christmas and the house was in a state of **anticipation.**
Everything was happening, but **relaxation!**

There was the tree to put up and **decorate,**
Cookies and cakes to **bake…**
There were programs to attend, trying not to be **late!**

Hang the wreath on the **door,**
And then off to the department **store!**

Gifts to buy, Gifts to **wrap.**
With all this activity,
What could they do but **laugh!**

This Christmas could not top the **last,**
But it would be as good as any they had in the **past!**

This brings me to the end of my **rhyme,**
But I believe for last minute shopping…
There is still **time!!**

…

(From "Rhymes for Christmas")

A Tribute to my Parents

Once upon a time, in a place very near **here,**
a girl and boy met and married…So I did **hear.**
After living here and there, they settled in a small house.
which had a river running **near.**

It was no time at all until the **house**
was a home with chickens, and a garden;
I even recall a **mouse.**

Pretty soon their family grew, and grew and **grew.**
As the years **flew;**
almost every year brought life **anew!**

As life went on in the little house, new ones came and older ones **left.**
And because of this, the two often times never really **met!**

Through the years a total of 14 children were born in **all.**
And by God's plan, they lost two children when they
were very **small.**

One day the wife gave birth to a little girl.
But this one was different for she was born in a hospital.
As luck would have it, this was their **last.**
They waited and watched them all grow as time quickly **past.**

Both grandchildren and great-grandchildren **came**
and that little house just put up with the **strain.**

One day it was time for the husband and father to rest.
After all, he had worked all his life;
A lot harder than all the rest.

The mother was lonely after he **passed**.
But she knew it was only a matter of time before
tomorrow would be her **last**.

Now they are both together **again**.
Young, Healthy, and Vibrant once **again**.

They look down on us each and every **day**,
and help us follow life's path in the right **way**.

They know that someday we will all be together **again;**
But not in a little house,
But in God's Heavenly Home **Instead!**

But until that time comes,
Let's all remember from where we came
And forever be **grateful**
that two young hearts remained forever **faithful!!**

(To my parents, I miss you still.)

...

(From "The 14th Child")

Mother's Alphabet

*A*lways answering your toughest questions.
*B*andaging your every cut or wound.
*C*aring for you and your brothers and sisters.
*D*oing many things to help you learn right from wrong.
*E*ncouraging you to try new things.
*F*inds new ways to help with a problem.
*G*ives attention to everyone.
*H*elps with math homework.
*I*s being an angel everyday and every week.
*J*umping with joy when you get good grades.
*K*isses you when you feel sad.
*L*ends a hand when you need it most.
*M*akes cookies so good you want to eat all of them.
*N*ever really gets mad at you.
*O*nly lets you eat sweets on holidays or special occasions.
*P*ays you for babysitting when Dad forgets.
*Q*uiets fights.
*R*eminds you to brush your teeth.
*S*ings you to sleep at night.
*T*ells the best fairy-tales ever.
*U*ndoes madness.
*V*entures with you through every problem.
*W*ants the best for you in the future.
*X*ex-perienced what you experience now.
*Y*ells your name with joy when you come back home after a long absence.
*Z*ip-zap, sometimes Moms say that.

...

(From "Rhymes for Our Serious Side")

Father's Alphabet

*A*lways answering your toughest questions.
*B*uilt you castles in the sand and igloos in the snow.
*C*arried you on his shoulders when you were too tired to walk.
*D*oing many things to help you learn right from wrong.
*E*xplained your schoolwork in a way you could understand it.
*F*atherhood is pretending the present you love most is soap-on-a-rope.
*G*uides you down the right path.
*H*elps you bait your fishing hook.
*I*s there to show you how to hit a baseball.
*J*udges you fairly.
*K*ills the monster under your bed.
*L*ends a hand when you need it most.
*M*akes adventures memorable.
*N*ever really gets mad at you.
*O*ffers advice when asked, but supported your decisions.
*P*retends not to laugh when you are crying over something silly.
*Q*uiets fights.
*R*eminds you that someday you too will have the hard job of being a parent.
*S*igns your permission slips.
*T*ucked you in at night and told you bedtime stories.
*U*ndoes madness.
*V*entures with you through every problem.
*W*ants the best for you in the future.
*X*ex-perienced what you experience now.
*Y*ields to Mother's wishes over his own when needed.
*Z*ip-up…That is something Dads remind their son's to do.

…

(From "Rhymes for Our Serious Side")

The End

Would you like to see your manuscript become a book?

If you are interested in becoming a PublishAmerica author, please submit your manuscript for possible publication to us at:

acquisitions@publishamerica.com

You may also mail in your manuscript to:

**PublishAmerica
PO Box 151
Frederick, MD 21705**

www.publishamerica.com